Intimate, low-voiced, delicate things

Intimate, low-voiced, delicate things

Esther Ottaway

PUNCHER & WATTMANN

First published in 2021
Published by Puncher and Wattmann
PO Box 279
Waratah NSW 2298

http://www.puncherandwattmann.com
puncherandwattmann@bigpond.com

NATIONAL
LIBRARY
OF AUSTRALIA

A catalogue entry for this book is available from the National Library of Australia.

ISBN   9781922571014

Cover image: *We are so lightly here* by Tasmanian artist Mandy Renard
Cover design by Miranda Douglas
Typesetting by Morgan Arnett
Printed by Lightning Source International

Contents

Inspiration

Lying beside my daughter as she sleeps
I listen to her hodgepodge bedtime sounds:
kitchen clatter, cars revving up the road,
the spooling hiss of a story cassette at its end.
Her stripling body is a tree, lips whispering
like leaves. I hear her stomach stirring milk,
her indrawn breath, think of its name: *inspire*.

She thrusts a hand out, holding back the dark,
flings a sapling arm across my neck.
Feet scuffle like mice in the sheets. Her eyes open
sightlessly, and look me in the face:
dark gaze of numen, fierce and strange as loss.
I hear the truth: the risk of life is death.
I have breathed her in; I can never breathe her out.

Roy, 1932

Mick and I break into bushmen's huts
hungry for bread or cake. We are never lost,

the bush and the stars have seeped into our feet.
Neither are we found. At home, our mother's welcome —

there you are you little blighters, a few hits with the stick.
We trap snakes, practise birdcall, suck at the teat

of someone's cow, follow a creek or a twist of cloud
for days. We sleep furled in the cold hearts of trees.

When I reach the team at each week's end
it's smoko. I am nine. I stand with the horses

as men gather packs, set out for weekends
of clamouring children, oven-hot stew,

the taut embraces of stalwart wives. My father
slaps my shoulder in passing, doesn't look back.

The crunch of their boots over leaf-litter fades,
there are only the sounds of the forest closing its fist.

I feed the horses; they all have shoes. My soles
run red, apprenticed to bracken and granite,

ants, razor-edged rocks, dry-ice frosts.
I pee on my freezing feet, clamber up a horse

to knead them under its mane's patchy blanket.
If ever I cry there are only the mares to hear.

The fire in the hut is dying again, the bush
hunching itself into the knot of night.

Soon enough I am broken in: tough as old boots.
I am a child workhorse, shod with scars.

ii

Along the dry creek-bed the log is gaining
on the hard-bitten shoe-horse.

My father shouts, fast and fricative,
time yawns open like the mouth of death:

a stone to feet of clay, the iron-shod log
grinds hoof and hock in a scream of chain.

He grips the victim's head,
speaks into her ear with a nurse's calm.

Perhaps he will take the needle from his kit
snap a long hair from her panicked tail

scald it in the billy, skirl boracic powder
into the wound, and stitch, the way I have seen him

stitch many horses, and his own injured body.
He does not. He reads in the mangled achilles

the limits of care brooked by death.
No exit from the bush except on one's feet.

He slits the jugular with a barking axe,
helps the horse lay down. I gather branches,

sit with my feet to the pyre's heat.
That night my father quickly snuffs

the lantern, orders sleep. In dreams he owns
a sunlit paddock, filled with broken horses.

iii

After two days I run away from school
and follow the well-worn track to the logging coupe.

I can read everything I need to
in the steep topography of Father's face:

his nose as straight and hard as a eucalypt,
the eyebrows' firm horizon, wide, bare paddock

of browbone, an extravagance of hair —
his fullness of yearning, tucked under his hat.

His face has hardened with each of the thirteen children
who grow inside our weary mother like weeds,

with each of the makeshift houses we live in and leave
as the logging team tracks further down the coast.

He is a field harrowed down to the stones.
Only his eyes are still soft as a yearling's

as he cradles the head of the horse he killed today,
as the iron vice of the bush clamps shut around him

and we read the spreading bloodstain in the dirt,
a map of some red-bright life he couldn't afford.

Liminal love songs

The way of an eagle in the heavens

Reflected in an eye, the dizzy paisley
of earth laid out for miles, the fiction
of early warning. Tallest bluff,
wind-chill written in the hunch of trees.

I cling to rock, stare at the arc
of wingspan longer than my body,
clutch at the theory of a home always
in this nest, this lover. Time

and unforeseen occurrence. Eggs
blotched like a hunter's moon. We kiss,
draw barbs and hooks to smoothness,
fit closer than feather. How long

can this slow pattern – caring,
paining, forgiving – take flight
and return? I trace the cliff
of your brow with my finger,

your temple's shallow chalice
the shape of a stick-raft nest
of exposure, the drop-edge
of cheekbone, imagine waking

beside you on the tallest
cliff, to the shock of height
and a hooked tongue, unable to tell you
I'm sorry. Below us, everything.

The way of a serpent on a rock

Come on then, sweet-skinned creature –
love's not one of the human rights
but something one learns

in the intricate sting
of shedding, addiction to skin
and pattern, each scale mirroring

the contour of its mate,
half-hidden, half-exposed, the memory
of my hair coming down in a certain light

coiled into the pocket of your heart.
Or instinct, the draw of sun-hot granite
to the slow belly, urge to roll back

the clenching cold; my hands
in a nest of questions. I cannot
grasp what makes a predator,

divide love from craving when we find
each other in the reptilian dark
of our separate selves,

eyes full of scales,
blood racing with sinuous hunger
to bite, to be swallowed whole.

The way of a ship in the heart of the sea

Hatchway of a vessel, the shower door
shudders on its runner, takes us inside

I face you under the hot hiss of water, skin
plumping like soaked fruit, exhaling

like leaves, wonder where in this water
we meet, what things your skin

might breathe to mine, what things are
washed away, and whether I could name

what familiarity erodes, or whether
these points of reference –

breakers of foam on your razor, smooth
river-stones of your shoulders, shining

whalebone of your hip – have slipped
into unconscious seas, and my skin is the fish

which no longer feels the waves, my senses
are faithless as sand, and this is why

I scribble charts of you, haul in shoals
of your words, sketch the precise drape

of sheet when you sleep, why my fingers
log the swell of a blue-soft vein, why,

when you tell me you love me
I sing to myself in the roiling dark:

I am in the heart of the sea
I am in the heart.

The way of a man with a maiden

You pluck a poinciana, walk me through humid rain
around your childhood block. Thank you,

you say, for coming here, and the flame tree's bloom
is a blood-rush to my cheek. I can't explain

why fertile chance delivered you to me,
why until this journey I have not acknowledged

your uprooting. In every story you are alone.
I tuck the flower behind my ear, stoop

to a kangaroo paw's black fist, send seeds
rattling like departing trains: clumsy on your trail

I make a mess of spoor, and can't tell
what it is that I have broken underfoot,

how to tread down the past. At the lawn's edge,
locked out of your home, you are as weary

as a man grown used to desert. I cling
to your hand, don't have the words you need.

In the hotel I stroke the petals' bruises,
mesmeric as wounds. Beneath the sheet

your hands   are the flower
         a displaced heart, aflame
you track me   seed me   tell me you will never
              go away

Chair on a high-rise balcony

Caught between the clouds and earth
the chair is perched like a bird.

You know the feeling, the vague distress
of legs far from the ground.

Sit in the chair. The balcony speaks
of parts of your life which hang by a thread;

like you, the chair is fine-boned
and without wings. Little choice now

but to go on believing
the logic you have engineered will hold.

Two heliotropes

for Kim

Your freckled face is evidence
in black-eyed daisies, gold as gold.
You follow my lens, a heliotrope.
Again, we seal the moment up –
picking threads from time's slick suit
and waiting for our lives to start,
we want the proof: something was good.
The daisies stink, but we're not here
for comfort – there's that shot of me
lying on a jetty in seagull-splatter,
the bathing suit glamorous as the future,
pinkie toe extended, just so. We're young
and flawless. The camera lies and lies.

For Mum on reading my poems

if you don't understand them don't worry don't try to worry your way
into them and take them apart as if you must apprehend meaning
don't try to follow them the way you would wounds on my body
instinctively blindly don't let yourself be hurt in the places I'm hurt
just because I've spoken of them because I know my pain is always
yours because I can't help but disorient you with the incomplete
inchoate maps I draw to find my way forward to name and stitch
together to lay to rest so while this is an exposure both of raw damage
and of love don't believe these are unhealed places the fact that I
speak of them means the suffering has eased and when I've needed
you I've called you to my side like the very early morning I lay on
the cold floor grieving while my daughter slept like the many times I
seemed unhappy unfixable unaware that each of these times opened
a corresponding wound in you now I step my way through things like
an adult clean up my own messes genuinely mostly cope so please take
these outcries as moments in the whole the numinous process and
understand that at each turn I've been steadied by this: your love.

Couple

When my mother spoke, he ignored her.
When she did not speak, he ignored her.
When she spoke of him, she called him *Your-father*
as if the fault were mine. It was mine, I knew,
because I loved him, and he would not love her,
and she could not love him; my love not enough
to mend it. I did bring them light,
they looked at me and saw some light
in my A's at school, my poems, my clumsy music
and they took it into their hearts that were starved of love.
I still say to them, look! I've been doing this, and this.

Absolution

Nineteen today and somnolent and absent
you trail like a driftnet. Kauri shell,
spotted, coiled in on yourself – I often wish
to hold you to my ear, confirming
your roaring remains cryptic, disturbing. Am I seeking
absolution? You're almost all the memories I have,
so many backyard bikes and questions of remorse –
did I reject too many fractions? I was never quite convinced
of your right to baggage, but then, nor by your
later black-eye excuses. You were ebbing away
for months, your unwashed hair too feral
for my business-suit dependencies. Did you think
I would not miss you? I have no hope of naming you,
but we are sisters, more each other than anyone.
Somewhere, you drift. I trail along the shore.

Every afternoon my father

Every afternoon my father drops in
and I make us a cup of tea.
If I've made cake, we eat some.
He's been fixing something vintage,
a boat or car or piece of furniture,
and tells me how he's crafted missing pieces
or thought up a cheaper fix.
I show him photos I've shot,
we talk about a documentary,
an exhibition. He has a joke to tell me
then he plays his guitar
and sings me songs he's written.
My daughter tells him her news
and when she's accidentally funny
he shoots me a jovial eyebrow.
He insists on mowing my lawn
though I have a gardener now.
He brushes down his overalls,
we have another cup of tea
and I read him my new poem.
I kiss him and send him off with a copy.
Of course, it was like this between us
more than a decade ago
before he stopped seeing me to prove a point.
These daily made-up visits
hold off the memory
of the furious darkness in his eyes.

Lipstick

for Auntie Jenny

When Mum offered me your lipstick
I took it, like a fool, thinking it was just
a lipstick, thinking I might make use of it —
we were never a family to waste things.
I pulled off the cap to check the colour:
a gentle pink I could wear with anything
and into my handbag it went. It's only now
in the morning rush in the chilly bathroom
as I press its shining cream along my lips
as its powdery scent releases and you come to me,
   standing on your tippy-toes
   to wrap your arms around my neck
   pressing your cheek soft with powder
   and wet with a visitor's tears against me
   my nose in the folds of your elegant scarf
   in the scent of clean linen as you say
   I love you so much, I'm sorry I can't be here more often
   and you kiss my cheek with this, this very lipstick,
it's now that, under my ribs, my disbelief that you have died
breaks, and I'm held in the mirror, soft-lipped, crying.

At the baby shower

I used to be a thin girl
thin   thin   thin
are you anorexic
said the high school girls

today the girls played a game
snipping pieces of string
guessing at the girth
of my fat fruit belly

how long is a piece of string?
how long can a girl stay thin?

Song for a neonate

You are light as a remark.
Your eyes, those of the unhomed,
are bright and human, perhaps beyond bearing.

In a distant room
your mother is a love song.
Hear her, over your own new symphony:
a lamb's-mew cry, a lapping tongue,
a slow dance of limbs against flannelette and air,
the weight of breath.

Take up your task. Search out her music
past incubator hum and trolley-wheel clatter:
the swoosh and thump of her heart's thrust,
salt and membrane, buoyancy, heat.
Through antiseptic and plastic tubing
nose out the hot scent of her milk —
she wills you, sings the strength of love.
Wake, remember. Your small warmth is a fire.

First blood

It was night, the telephone
rang, I walked down to the shed
the baby in my arms
but never made it, falling slowly,
the hard fact of the concrete path
loud in my mind, wishing so much
for grass or water or sand, but knowing
just the concrete gunning for us, the concrete bare
as the baby's head, and I came down hard
on bended knee, my arms
lifting the offering of her,
round fruit of her head
in beseeching hands,
knowing my weight
would pitch us forward
and as my arms hit the concrete
and I felt her head whip through my hands
and smack the path, I cried out and understood:
I was going to fall down on this job,
and we both were going to bleed.

Broken glass

Through the bubbled, stippled
nineteen-fifties surface, the dark cracks spiked
like an asterisk outwards to the frame.

Peering harder
into the once-fashionable glass
obfuscated for front-door privacy,

one sees it's useless for the purpose,
making the owner transparent
while strangers remain obscure. I'll confess

those mismatched panes were part of the charm
of the stolid house, as we stood on the porch
heady with first-home owners' grant:

bubbly glass, glasses of bubbly,
brisk new-place promises – redo the meterbox,
pitch the venetians, and first thing

replace this broken glass. So the old,
clear packing tape retained its dusty grains
of sunlight-perished glue, held the mess together

for three and a half years, until the baby crawled.

~

The baby is Icarus
drawn to every floor-level, disastrous sun –

oven, power points,
rubbish bin, the three-pronged end
of the vacuum cleaner's cord

which pops neatly into her mouth,
flex trailing between lips like a lit fuse –
and the low, cracked pane. A hand the width

of packing tape reaches up,
leans on the glass, tests, rests weight
while the other swings from carpet

to bang on the surface – we fly
and scoop, remonstrate pale-faced
with ourselves. My father comes to stay:

we ought to knock that pane out,
losing count of my leaps. *Got any tape?*
Won't match that surface, though – too old.

I hand him packing tape, scissors,
hover anxiously. The sound
of the tape ripped from its spool

makes baby cry and cling.
I whisk her off to the cot's safety,
don't look, full of visions

of the falling shards
despite Dad's tape, glittering, burrowing
like scorpions. They're icebergs. Mines.

The surgery goes well. Dad carries off
the flexing, edgy mat, and he's long gone
when I find one tooth-sized fragment

sharper than any shark's incisor.
Held to the light, its smoothest surface dips
in precise convex. I wrap it,

shove it deep in the bin,
vacuum the carpet, vacuum it again,
vacuum the concrete porch —

that's what glass does
to me, broken glass
beds in like risks,

lodging slyly who knows where.
There's always one to dagger you
when you've forgotten —

dawn-smudged, padding out in pyjamas
to make a cup of tea,
grab the phone, answer the door,

stabbed. I answer the door:
it's Dad, triumphant. Glinting.
An offcut. *There's enough down there*

to do the whole porch! My pause.
It's OK, Dad; if you fix the cracked one
I'll be happy.

It'll only take a minute, love.
Look so much better. Leaning
on my glass. He doesn't know

how badly taped I am
since giving birth, how insular.
Can't watch the news. My incubus:

fear in an eggshell. Trying
to keep a lid on things. Ain't broken,
don't fix it – can't stomach

another hammer-swing,
fragments showering, bedding in
who knows where, close to the bone.

~

The accident wouldn't have happened
had I not cooked us a hot dinner
(at dinnertime, more's the wonder)

and plated it just as the last of
baby's attention span ran out.
Bring her in here then,

she can play on the lino. Plonking the box
of Tupperware between her splayed legs,
we turned back to our cooling plates.

The two glass jars were buried,
potbellied deep in the box, and curved snugly
into her new-minted palms

and the smash as she brought them together
was clean, a single, musical shatter.
Picture three of us frozen, chilled,

the moment knocked flat like a photograph.
The jagged spikes gleaming in her hands,
the glistening lapful.

The blood I saw
tracking down her thin wrists
was not real, not real, I had her wrists

safe, clamped in my fingers,
safe, as my husband eased the blades
from her grip, the not-there blood

bubbled faster, she dripped, eidetic screaming
riddled me, the shaking started
in my legs. We stood her up

in the heavy near-miss silence,
picked off the glitter, peeled away like paramedics
the glinting, loaded jumpsuit.

~

On TV late that night
a man eats a martini glass.
As he wraps his lips and cheek-pockets

carefully, awkwardly, around the pieces,
crunches molars down and swallows,
I know precisely how the fragments feel

against his tongue,
this concave surface smooth and sure,
then the razor's edge. This is a trick

I have to practise,
don't know how
to swallow it:

risk,
inhabiting the mother-brink.

The stars

pale spots of lichen on bitumen
my toddler leads me
walk on the stars?

A fistful of suns

Instinctively watchful, cat from a box, I am nosing
down the bridle track from the foreign house to the road.
As if I have somewhere to go, as if I can find you.

The white-cloud sky could blind me, the air holds water
against the redolence of wet-stone moss and leaf rot.
A long-beaked native dips into the cleft nectary
of a red bottlebrush, the thin limb bouncing
under its featherweight. Through a sweep of sclerophyll
briar roses run in magenta smears.
Indigenous creepers tangle with holly, wild honeysuckle,
where I wander with my zipped-up body heat.
On the bend there is a gift: massed yellow daisies
as big as your baby fists, petal-ends serrated into four points.
They stop me in my tracks, razzle-dazzle,
God's concert for a music-starved heart.

I uproot the first one, ascertain the knack
of snapping stalks at the dichasium,
preserving the root. Up to my knees
in a pigment bath, I pick quickly,
a child lost to a buttermilk breast.
I win a fistful of suns. Recalling my mother's method,
I choose some greenery, a bracken frond:

in the vase flowers bob about, spurning arrangement.
Their chromotherapy infuses, firms me.
They are eighteen of your faces, bright with living;
suns which promise they will rise,
one by one by one,
            until I see you again.

Notebook and daughter

she is drawing smiley faces
at the end of my words
pink faces to make it pretty
she is kissing my cheek

at the end of my words
I curl my arm around her
she is kissing my cheek
those lines of love and worry

I curl my arm around her
before the world can write on her
those lines of love and worry
she says *you've got two more lines*

before the world can write on her
pink faces to make it pretty
she says *you've got two more lines*
she is drawing smiley faces

Triptych

My daughter explains how it happened: *Grandma is your mother.*
The same sapphire eyes, set in the frames of our ages, from a line
of Irish genes: a series of sketches, as if the edges
of each of us are uncertain, our bodies
a triptych, attempts at the same idea. When
the idea of my daughter began sculpting my self-

image, I was as shocked as if I had been born with *self*
tattooed on my belly and now saw the letters ballooning: mother
in the making, wary of the crossing – less a borderline
than a no-man's land between selfhood and the mythic edge
of the world, over which women named *mothers* had fallen. Their bodies
tried to explain, in foreign tongues thick with milk, how it would be when

I split like a fruit and shivered at my baby's cry, or when,
a revenant, I would begin to remember myself.
When she opened her tiny sapphire eyes, I wanted my mother
to be the first to see her. I shone like a jewel, fulcrum in a line
of matriarchs, unaware that I'd been edged
out of the present. My mother held her, their bodies

slotting together, genes in a double helix, as the bodies
of my mother and myself did once, and I visioned her when
she sat in that hospital bed, her self
slipping away; as if from being a mother
we thought there was hope of return. Any line
separating us, any edge

between us burned away, and freed from edges,
linked with every woman and their bodies,
I plunged into the selfless dream. Today, I am found out when
my small daughter rages: *I will do it myself!*
I can't stop my practised hands, the hands of a mother,
from fastening shoes or brushing hair; she pushes them away, a line

drawn between us, firm as those furrowed lines
of determination on her forehead, primal as the edge
of consciousness. And I see she has to love and hate me, our bodies
driven to fight suffocation. I turn bitter when
she says from her car seat *I don't need you any more, Mum* – can't stop
    myself
trying to sully her clarity: sharp-tongued, I say *I still need my mother*

and I'm grown up. Everyone needs their mother. I weave through the line
of traffic, recall screaming at my mum, pushing her to the edge. Our bodies
speak truth: what I say to my daughter, I say to my mother, myself.

her childish singing
all the sweeter
for being temporary

Daughter in a darkened room

Sleeping, she carves trails in the air.
Her hands rise and fall, her head turns,
working at her delicate night writing.
She mouths its silent language
as if we both can see, as if I could decipher it. I watch
as it dissolves above her, her fingers
flaring, reaching. I wish for her
that over her are the names of those she loves.

Yes, she looks so much like me

and yes, she's the gone girl and greenhorn of me
and yes, she's the hilarity and henpeck of me
and yes, she's the codswallop and melee of me
and yes, she's the gavel and mercenary of me
and yes, she's the baggage and shortfalls of me
and yes, she learns and loans me
and yes, she rules and reels from me
and yes, she flames up and is saddled with me
and yes, she's the oasis and oath of me
and yes, she's the prophet and pride of me
and yes, she'll be the death of me.

Serenity prayer at thirty-four

I have returned my can of hairspray to its holster.
I am letting my hair fall in strange directions.
Is this the serenity to accept what I cannot change,
the courage etcetera etcetera, my self-esteem
wrestling the media onslaught and finally winning?
Or the birth of a slackness I should find alarming,
that leads to wearing slippers to the corner shop, and thence
to wandering through the park, my thin nightie
open, muttering poetry, trailed by cats?
If I told my old friends it's getting harder
to fight the feeling that I'm actually ugly,
they'd laugh. A teenager would understand, perhaps.

Sonnet for stages

She drives me mad with YouTube videos.
They're in a giant bowl of cereal!
I try to pay attention, strive to smile
that way that each attentive parent knows,
that way we feign delight when babies' paws
will push their half-sucked biscuits through our lips,
when they style our hair with bows and clips
or when at eight they're thralled by dinosaurs.
At every stage, they seem forever-bright,
but stages die. I remember when
Auntie Cath enlightened me one night:
Some weeks feel like they will never end,
but the years go quickly. She was right.
Come here, my love; let's watch that clip again.

Night on my own, Yarra River

Ferries glide by, trains go at appointed minutes.
My coffee cools. I have the luxury of long thoughts,
the state of aloneness as foreign as the place.
A clock still set to the hours of my child
I track her movements, text at the right times,
feel the strange untethering of letting go.
No one is waiting for me, no one
dependent on the high wire of my actions –
I keep checking, have I got time? And I know
before the day I drink in the sweet sorrow
of empty nesting, time is a river flowing away.

Two letters

dashed, torn
down one edge, folded
three times, corrected
once, two closing
effulgences,
two kisses,
one by-
the-way.
I missed
the love-dash
of you.

~

texture like the down
on a face. Poetry spooled out,
sparely punctuated, ruminant,
taking me deep on the dive — a hooked fish
flashing knife-silver down, down,
free-finning through your words' waterspout
till the throat-drag begins to tell,
homes me out in mid-arc slow motion:
now pulled, now swimming,
now trawled, lifted, gasping,
flying silver-limned in the sea sun.
I shook my head, felt fear, beauty.

Light, water

The sleep I've missed throbs in my head.
The driver coughs asthmatically, the coach sways like a womb
past bright canola, Tas-Ag Services,
the burnt-out ruins of a house, front windows
framing nothing. And everywhere spilt water,
pooling in dark button grass,
flashing with brief gleams of sky,
the mercury ideas of the heart.
There is an ache behind my ribs for you.

Campbell Town, Ross, Oatlands, Kempton,
paddocks, makeshift memorials to the dead.
The headrests of the seats in front
frame the bare shoulder of a man,
muscles and hollows, skin the shade of sand.
I want to lean forward, put my nose
to the soft heat of its smell,
kiss it with gentle lips, the way I might kiss
a baby's forehead, in reverence for beauty.
But it would be your shoulder,
your scent as intimate as clothes,
its fine oiled surface like chamois to my cheek.

The sky spins backlit cirrus clouds
in a powder burst of pinks and blues –
a bunny-rug laid over sleeping lambs –
then sucks the day's last breath
and all the grass looks cold.
Lights come on in villages like candles.
When I get home you will be out at work.
You will have thought to leave the porch light on.
I will nose around our house putting things in place,

put on pyjamas, put myself to bed.
You will come home when I am sleeping,
kick off your good shoes, bang the wardrobe door,
roll into bed. I will tuck my hands against your chest
and put my feet on your feet, and breathe
and dream of miles in dark quicksilver water.
In front of me the man puts on his coat;
the coach gears back, climbing the long hill home.

Days look on love

as cake looks on
embroidered cloth:
archaic, exquisite against
days' increments of gritty
street litter, endearments
stand as lovely baskets
brought in from the rain,
ovened, warming round
kitchen-stained flagstones,
retained as souvenirs or
filaments turned on
when each day's sun
begins to cool.

Ocean nocturne

A vinegar sky, the moon with its mouth full of cloud.
My words arrive in a squall of leaves, my silences
knotted as dragnets. You gather them up,

trusting the eyes of your hands with these difficult signs.
How to keep faith in love's instinct, the senses translating
the tangled regrets of a lover, the tongue sharp as flax?

Our bed is a refugee raft on a black heart of water.
The surge of your body shuts out the mute moon
and its questions, your shadow is sedative.
I take you in, on an ocean deep as need.

Love: a misunderstanding

Some days you shouldn't be trying, as if
while you were in it the goodnight scene in the restaurant
gravitated toward Australian soap
easing your voices into the slight tinniness
of second-rate sound recording, subtly retouching the blander colours
to compensate for the peeling woodgrain, and in so doing
distanced you from your own part, so that even as you speak
it's difficult to be convincing.

Like something that didn't arrive with the coffee, you're missing
all the interesting bits, trying to be captivating
until exquisitely witty lines and spontaneous laughter
swallow much too much attention and again you're curiously outside
    yourself,
accepting a glittering photograph of your dinner companion
and wondering why you're bothering –

days when you don't notice bubbles of speech
shooting straight past Wernicke's area of the brain,
mimicking the feeling of talking to yourself;
going home five percent miffed, you realise he did tell you
tonight you looked beautiful, but, exhausted by your efforts
and obsessed with whether or not the door was
sliding, you just weren't around to notice.

Letters at forty

As though I could articulate what's happened – as though
baying about betrayal and
circumstance and an unravelling marriage will help –
daily in my head I write to Christiana,
elaborately forming ways to ask
forgiveness for my absent friendship,
graceless around my faults, choked with
half-baked explanations, unable to account for times
I said I'd call, or visit: those promises
jokes from behind illness and loneliness,
kidding myself I'd feel fine tomorrow, the next day.
Look at the writer, who can't construct a sentence.
My husband spends his time with someone else.
Nervous, loveless and, as my daughter tells me,
older than Nintendos, I'm wearing high heels again,
parodying girlhood, used to sleeping alone under our
queen-sized doona – God said *love her as yourself,* and those
reminders of our hopeful early marriage
seem to smash me whole some nights, Christi –
those talks on loving the cherished vessel
upending the china cabinet of my heart. Everything is
vanity, Solomon said, and went on collecting woman after
woman: he saw his faults, and they still killed him. Each year the
x-ray traces fault-lines in my breasts. What can I do? I write, pray to
Yahweh, grow tomatoes, befriend anyone who says
zounds! Still have some spark in me. And I miss seeing you.

it's not when we tell her
but when you move your things out
that our daughter cries

How are you?

I'm the photos that can't be looked at
I'm the fool before his friends

I'm the worn step of the family home
I'm the silence after the strangling

I'm the calm emergency procedure
I'm the packer of children's suitcases

I'm the hoarder's religion of objects
I'm the pusher of wheelie bins

I'm the vinegar when the wine has turned
I'm the good mother's dark nights

I'm the roadside mess, the pouch still wriggling
I'm the woman with nothing to say

Prescience

for Sylvia Plath

I understand you
curled in that crawl-space
under your mother's house,
filled with pills.

You lie in the black
mouth of your living body
trying to marry peace
before your husband can betray you.

He will leave both of us
as if we were mistakes,
one a fool, the other a fool.
We'll bite down on our hearts.

Pain is readying for us.
I knew it when, as a child,
I used to stop breathing
for the peace, the peace.

Halfway through their Gold Coast holiday

I wake from the humiliation dream,
where all his friends know he's leaving me
but no one tells me, then I realise
that while I spoke of healing they were laughing.
Of course, it really happened, at that wedding —
he held my hand and led me to the buffet
and let me talk of reconciliation,
watched me dance with a man who'd taken pity.
The nausea stays all day, the self-love quotes
all impotent, his vows raw in my body.
Tonight he lies between her sheets and mine,
his happiness a blade pressed to my throat.

Crochet in autumn

This is the season when I have to pay
for my long summer light, my latitude.
The short days ask too much. The house
is not home, the bed not free of memories.
I'm single, and I cannot speak of it
but through the woman's work my dumb hands reach for —
unlikely soothing: laying out small nooses
again, again, to hush each minute, wring its endless neck.

Best mate

After a year
why did you hug me?
Standing on my porch, a sudden grasp and cheek-kiss.

Did you
    think because I made the conversation exes make
    I'm feeling happy?

    want assurance that you're okay with me?
    (you're not okay with me)

    read my face, a place you've known by heart
    and tell I'd been writing of pain?

    know I've started grieving at night again?

    sense forgiveness spawning in my waters,
    one part per million?

    feel sad over me
    or guilty over something you're about to do?

That firmly platonic energy
as though you were hugging a best mate.
I went inside and cried on our child.

Valuation

Through his lens he scrutinises
my diamond-studded rings.

I think of what they mean
and what they didn't mean.

Had enough of them?
The air in the tiny workshop
flames in my lungs:

just history, I say.

*I'll unceremoniously
chop them up,* he says.

I want to kiss the rings goodbye,
press my lips
to the younger self who had faith.

Without a ceremony
I leave
half a carat lighter.

Great egret

Reading a field guide, I find myself:
tall, graceful, long-necked white bird.
I like you, egret
because you're almost *regret*, yet you are not regret,
as *to egress* is not *to regress* —
though haven't I struggled to know that,
unable to go back or go on.

The wing beats are slow and deliberate.
Usually feeds alone, standing motionless
at the kitchen counter, reliving a tragic love
or slowly stalking insects in shallow water
because who has the courage for deep water now?

Now, I will learn to be you —
graceful, making a slow and deliberate egress
from what I almost, but not quite, regret.

Coming home

I asked her to use the back door —
the key's sound in the front
is too long a memory.

I don't know how
to share a house
without sharing a bed, a child.

> We have started
> *tabemono o kyoyu suru:*
> to share food.
>
> She has stubborned her way past
> my litany of allergies,
> studied me when I'm cooking.
>
> She thinks in food, takes photos,
> delivers to friends.
> I come home to new smells.

I remember slick ramen
street-side in Fukuoka,
pork broth and fatty back,

the teppanyaki we thought was eight dollars
but was eighty — I was never one
who could see the cost of things.

> She feeds me five-spice potato.
> My freezer fills with lace-edged dumplings,
> my bench with a rice cooker.

That love had been Fukuoka castle,
the walls soothing, the crushed-grass fragrance
of tatami. In Fukuoka,

the first place outsiders set foot,
he cast me away
in some hot and rainy garden.

I hadn't learned from the Yakui river-gate,
placed obliquely to prevent attack.
And when it came, I knew only
that self-destroying typhoon: the *kamikaze*.

I feel, like a blind woman,
for edges.
I rebuild, as the samurai,
laboriously,
my ramparts, sanctum.

> In place of his footsteps
> the swoosh of her slippered feet.

I relearn
my spirit's dimensions.
I find I like them.

> She rewrites my house's wedded soundscape —
> blasts her blender and deep fryer,
> sings songs from Asian musicals.
> When I cook mediocre *karaage*
> she praises my efforts.

I learn
to have a friend in my home
not an enemy.

                                        She buys the biggest cabbage
                                                I have ever seen;

I draw a face on it,
dress it in hats.
Day by day, I'm coming home
to myself.

                                        She makes soup of the cabbage
                                                and gives thanks for it —

and I give thanks
for the surprise of my own strength —
                itadakimasu:
                I humbly receive this.

Sonnet for fifteen

For all those years you couldn't leave me alone –
talked through the toilet door, climbed up my hips,
broke things, spilt things, cried help; now your headphones
kill conversation dead. You've stitched your lips.
Demanding answers for your million queries
seems finished now, and some emerging ego
has named you child-woman. The balance varies:
you earn a wage, and with it you buy Lego;
you wear lipstick, and when you make an error
at work, you cry, pale-faced with first-time fright.
Pushed off my pedestal, my role is mirror
or paramedic to your maiden flight.
It kind of hurts, but still I'll see you through.
You don't want me – except for when you do.

A nice man

When the old man in the shop queue gives her lollies,
I read simple kindness in his eye.
We say thank you, but I'm silenced
by my toddler exclaiming
that was a nice man! That experiment:
a man telling kids a puppy lived in his van
while their mothers watched in a secret room:
all the kids hopped in. The mothers were bawling,
riven like the bereaved. I say to Kim
did your father ever talk to you about men?
No, she says. And neither did mine. I thought
all men were lovely. And now my daughter's sixteen
and out there is an old man, or a young man,
a man who's vile and violent, a man who's nice.

Hope of escape

*Commissioned by Tasmania's Festival of Voices, this stage performance
piece includes verbatim quotes from diaries in my family history and
interviews with African women.*

1854

Leave the grey light of a foggy morning
Leave the lemon tree you planted together
Leave your favourite books lying on a chair
Leave the wooden rocking horse your children love
Leave the pillow your mother stitched for your wedding
Leave the soft lilting language of your people
Leave the green land that used to feed you
Leave your little sisters braiding their hair
Leave your nan in the workhouse
Leave your husband frozen in the ground

**Notice to Young Women, desirous of bettering their condition by
an Emigration to the Australian Colonies**: Every Arrangement will
be made for the Comfort of the Emigrants during the Voyage, and
Medical Assistance provided. They will also be taken care of on their
landing in the Colonies; and they will find there, ready for them, a
choice of Employment and Wages.

Four thousand miles
from Hobart Town.
Very heavy snow on deck
knee deep in places.
Piercingly cold and dark all day.
The sailors light lamps
so that we can see to sew.

Some dolphin.
The sea a still pond.
We must sail on for months.
The world is bigger than anyone can imagine.

A sea so rough, we risk the deck for air.
The girls' hands clamped in mine, William behind,
I jostle through the passengers crowding out
and he's out of my sight when we reach the iron rail.
Gulping the blessed air, I scan for his head.
The scream is the most awful rending sound
     we are all stopped for a moment, struck
then calling voice after voice – a child is overboard.
I run. I fold the girls' hands onto that rail
and I run across the bucking, dripping deck
through waves of mothers, torrents of mothers, all calling
their young, mouths open, eyes white, fierce with rage.
We are nesting birds; the eagle has already struck.

They carry him by our berth, where my three huddle.
The child is whiter than eggshell and looks as frail
against the sailor's chest, his breeches sodden,
his new shoes for the journey still laced on.
The doctor and the father nearly fight over him
as they strip his clothes and rub him with flannel and brandy,
the warm bath ready, if he would but cry.
At four o'clock the bell tolls for the funeral.
The body has been sewn up in a canvas,
sand put at the feet to make it heavy.
I think no one could ever forget the sound
when the body drops into the deep.

We are by the gangway when suddenly all the water in God's earth
breaks over the ship. I am deafened by the great froth of water, the

bulwarks are washed away, water pours down on all of us below deck, the ship heaves so much that two women are thrown down onto tables, the screams are awful of women and children. The water has pushed my family back like little rag dolls and sucked them into a corner, thank the Lord they are all together, blinking like creatures as the water drains off them and crying. One woman has got her arm broken and another three ribs broken. The food swept from us, and the weather still so rough we cannot get anything more until Monday morning. I swear I have learnt to value the comforts of home, if it should please God to give me one again.

Very, very cold. Some snow has fallen and hail. Bruises coming up on the children. A cup of tea today is worth double what it was before. Service twice today, and after the storm, thanksgiving. In the night, we have had one birth on board. A girl, by the mother of the child that was drowned. I am miserable and sickened of a life at sea.

2010

Leave the River Nile full of shallow boats
Leave the pots of drinking water outside the houses
Leave the sweet milk at the roadside stall
Leave the henna tattoos on the married women's fingers
Leave the rain swelling over the drought
Leave the women winnowing corn into their laps
Leave the hot town spreading into the desert
Leave your little brothers running with hoops of tyres
Leave the Nubian man with the face of a king
Leave your love lying in the mouth of war

In the camp the queue is long as a trance,
dull as the sun's slow progress. I shamble and kick,
feet hardening through the holes in my shoes.
A scoop of semolina, a scoop of salt in my bag

and I am skipping back, quick as a goat
when I come up against the grubby soldier.
His chest roadblocks my face. His uniform reeks
of sweat and rice, dirty hands, smoke.
Give me your bag, he says. *I can get you out.*
I fix my eyes on my shoes, the places where
the edges peel away, like shoots of grass.
I help with the visa. Give me your bag. His hand
snakes round my arm. I give the bag up slowly,
as if it were a child, watching fiercely
as he passes it into his hand, his shirt. He grins,
good girl, and is gone. I stand there sickly,
grasping at nothing. He has put words in my hands.
I will feed them to my sister,
dust and words. I will eat them till I choke.

My sister born after me is called my follower.
When she cries because only we are left
I wrap her in my robe
and tell her, we will go to that place Australia.
We will have a house, a job,
grow up and drive a car
and we will get rich. I will be buying her everything,
every food and toys.
Those boys tell me Australia, it's bad,
they kill all their blackfellas a long time ago.
But I am not frightened. I have seen that place
on the DVD the UN lady show us.
Brick houses. Kangaroo on the street.
Near that Sydney bridge it's sunny and warm.
For seven years I tell my sister this story.
One morning the lady comes saying
the visa, the bus is coming
and on that paper I read a name. One name.

As the bus goes rattling away from my sister, my follower,
I watch her growing smaller through the window,
small enough to fit inside my heart.

In Cairo city there is no work.
I tell my boys, look in the street
for Coke bottles that are empty.
I stand in the hot kitchen,
stir the drum filled with sesame seed,
make the alcohol to sell it.
Baby Mafu is sitting on the floor,
her legs around an old tin
banging one hand on the lid.
I tell the boys, you watch for those police.
Because in Muslim law no alcohol,
if the police is coming in my house,
they are looking everything, finding alcohol,
I go to jail with the baby. This is women's work.
When my boys cry because they are hungry
I wrap them in my robe
and tell them We will go to that place Australia.
You will have a house, a job,
grow up and drive a car
and you will get rich.
For five years I tell my boys this story.

*

I have been stuck on this ship I have been stuck in Cairo city *all of my
life* forever. *The children call* children call and cry *they ask for water,*
more water, we are burnt by the sun *frozen by the rain, their clothes
and blankets all are soaked* their clothes are dusty, we sleep in one
blanket and it smells in here *and it smells, it is no place fit to care for
children* it is very hard to grow your kids, *I speak to the overseer* I go to

the UN every day *every day but he says he has nothing else to give me*
he has nothing else to give me, *and I must throw our miserable lot upon*
God because I have no power. I have to wait, I have to wait and hope
there will be something for us, *some change, some way of getting out of*
here
some way of not going mad
some hope of escape.

*

1854

A sailor cries *a boat, a boat*
all strain the eye to see
and narrowly we watch until the black spot on the water
comes nearer. If there never was a thankful heart before
there is now when the pilot steps on board.
And now many boats are coming up the stream
with people to enquire for their friends.
The great anchor is cast.

I do not well know what is best to do. I trust that Providence will
direct me for the best, for I have none here either to care for or
assist me. The Crown "accommodates" us for one night, in a lumber
yard. Then turns us out into an empty street, telling us to "engage
ourselves" to employment. I assure you it is quite requisite in this
Colony to have someone to uphold you. If you have not, you are looked
upon with contempt. I know what old Britain is. A fine place for the
rich, but the Lord help the poor. I know I would not go back again.
How to be broken, live in two places at once.

2010

I do the interview, the medical.

I go on five flights.
I didn't see a plane before.
I am feeling kind of miracle.
I'm full of religions, you know.
They give me a unit under a house.
It is dark and cold.
Letters come from Centrelink.
I think the letters are saying
they will come and take the unit.
Pauline Hanson comes to Hobart.
There is one channel on the TV.
It is playing *Australia's Most Wanted*.
If I go outside, blackfella woman, they will kill me.
I hide myself in bed.
The alphabet hammers at me.
I carry tribes in my mouth.
How to be broken, live in two places at once.

At the supermarket

Her adolescent hands take up my groceries.
In careful English she says *It is warm today*

and I see the scar that straddles her char-dark forehead.

Its length is chilling: there is no refusing
the machete's image, the *thunk* and force of the blow.

Yes, I say, and lift my bags to leave:
my heart cleft open, filling with this day's warmth.

A forked silent tongue

Lomandra longifolia

spiny-headed mat-rush
sewn into an alphabet

letters twisting, resisting
the weaver's flat-press

repelling the act of naming
dodging the dangerous label

baby basket, fish trap, eel trap, cape
coffin, egg-scoop, sister-basket, winnower

weed out, eliminate, eradicate
root out, stamp out, remove

touch the rush's tip
its forked silent tongue

all the things we name
    weed
        foreigner

knotted in stereotype
as if *to name* was *to know*

the mat-rush unfurls its own letters
put your hands in this poem of sand

question mark of a dolphin's spine
coil of a newborn's ear

spiral staircase of a seashell
calligraphy of endurance

let go of what you never needed
be an alphabet released

awake to the scent of grasses
less language   more love

the silence of your body
life-work, letter to the earth

read the veins of fibre
it is all right

to be unfinished
unexplained

it is all

Blazer

At all times, you will have on your hat, your gloves, your blazer.
—Mrs Burke, Deputy Head, Ogilvie High School, Black Tuesday, 7 February 1967

girls scatter from the hall beetles smoked from their nest
the sun is a black seed in a blood orange
the male teachers gone the women shooing us out
as I reach the path the fringes of the oval combust
and all the safety buckles of the world burn off me
I am walking in my hat my gloves my blazer
through the hearth of my own fear
my breath jagged with woodsmoke and sweat
my small arm pinioned under a bag of first-day books
on creek road one whole verge is on fire
fire that dad sets in the hearth of the living room
or for cracker night bonfire marshmallows and singing
how can the sky the road be fire the air
this wind catches me like a demon's hand I am running
please I have to get to my house my cry sucked into cinders
I am Gretel in the oven scratching the glass
my house his hands my matchstick legs my hat my gloves my blazer

How are you? (ii)

since her death
when I say it
I know how you are

devastated

my space probe
launched into raw territory

what you say back
though the words change
means

yes
there is
devastation

I say it
knowing we both know
the space is vast
years
in the traversing

I say it
so that
      when a faint signal
      starts to ping back
I will be there
listening

When I meet the painter

he is standing in the gallery
lone tree on a polished-concrete beach.
Too-short jeans, bushwalking boots,
the shirt of a quiet man.
I've just come in to sign a couple.
He kneels before a freezing sea
and as he mixes Belgian black
tells me about the faces of cliffs
where native flora clings,
gripping the edge of starvation
streaked by water seepage
battered by wind and salt.
It was a battle getting these together.
My wife had depression, my sons'
marriages broke up, I had to put
both my parents into homes
I had to really regiment myself.
Soldier and commander, locked in a shed
with visions of looming cliffs and massing cloud.
On the floor he takes apart a folder
in a last-minute flurry of papers.
It's getting better. Struggling to close the binding
he grins at himself – *I've got it upside down* –
and a laughing sky dawns in his eyes like love;
his crow's-feet wrinkles are all the rays of the sun.

Binalong Bay 2005: a Tasmanian demography

surprise! around this coast-twist
here's Melbourne and Sydney, run away —

priced out of their urban sprawl, poor things,
they're whooping and throwing sand in handfuls:

cheap waterfront! Picking our way around
the coast we observe, like age or divorce,

one of those things we stupidly
never saw coming: its empty S-bends

are scored with grey-clay driveways, spidered
into ugly skeletons, soon to be fat-fleshed

with uglier two-storey villas. This feels
like a common-law breach — don't they know

the beach should be ours? Howled down
by Market Forces, my shack-fantasy vanishes

like last light on a block of auctioned coast.
Yet it's our fault: we left our run too late,

you can see us grinning on the eighties postcard
titled Apple Isle — Where Nothing Changes,

knocking back $8000 beachfront fibro
because, cursed with genetic travel-avoidance,

we won't commute. That's me
leaning against the packing shed, exclaiming

"all the way to *Scamander?*"

City Sights Plus Dandenongs in Half a Day

falling for the gloss of tourist numbers
here's Mum's suitcase and me, jammed in the front seats
like schoolgirls with Jean from New Zealand,
who's eighty-six, she's told me, twice. We're whipped
around some Melbourne blocks – Parliament House,
a glimpse of the backside of stands
at the MCG. Here, though,
is the promoter's joke on the girl from Tassie:
I goggled till we left the six-lane highway
but now, gear-grinding up the mountains,
am bored: it's just bush.
The rosellas we pile out to feed are same-old
and, trained for commerce, not as endearing
as the thinner backyard variety. With Jean's Hanimex
I snap at the bickering pair on her head
as the honey-throated guide calls us to billy tea,
stirring at a blackened paint tin and elucidating
the singular aroma the gum leaf adds.
Young Singaporeans and Dutch retirees
sip and grimace. I pass. The guide's glib voice
warns gravely that Vegemite is not chocolate
as Dick Smith's loaded polly-want-a-crackers
are tested like grenade pins between neat Asian teeth.
I wish I had placards: *Toast, Not Crackers.* Always
I've been an awkward tourist – seeing, but never getting
the euphoria I paid for. The problem is,
someone's left all these Getaway Moments
out in the weather. I could come clean,
admit that I'd rather see a gallery than a glacier:
is that wrong? It feels as though
greater interest in the landscape of the mind
short-changes the seven wonders

though probably it's only sweet-talking tour operators
who feel the pinch. What's left to do
but pick the teeth of the tourism dream
on the long drive back to the lying poster?

West Terrace and Hindley Street

Traffic gripes like a stack of invoices. At the lights
a bag of empty Coke cans wrestles an old man for his scooter
and wins. The Adelaide Symphony plays Café:
variation on diminished funding. A blotchy baby's
pram jostles ours. A pot of beer
leans blearily against a mural. Rain
drops in. We duck into a bookshop's
hush. Tiger lilies prowl. Nudes lie.
The pram wheels squeak. My baby plays
Oh My Darling Clementine for a dark German.
A book asks politely *Are you left eyed?*
The cracked sky blisters into blue. We revolve
onto the street. Doorways steam. Galleries sprout.
Maple leaves freestyle. Young men
become beautiful. A pierced lover's crewcut
is cleft, blonde brain, brunette brain.
Chic cafés chrome. Construction bangs on
about why it's justified. A stick figure
pleads for three dollars for a hospital-baby.
Skaters scribble on the sky.
The air is freshly squeezed,
  lime, jasmine rice, sun,
the fringe flopping down into the eyes of the mainstream.
I could hang with the literati, dye my hair, take a lover.

As we pass the pokies lounge a woman
lays her head down on the bar,
her nicotine-yellow hair fanning out
in a riddle of roads less travelled.

Airplane poems

He charges like a kid with a kite
       (remember that flat-out adrenaline head,
       sound of sneakers, full pelt, slapping the tarmac?)
We're up and saved, and he throws us
into a generous, rolling turn like a champagne smile.
Thunderheads applaud. This fun is art.

My window,
crowded with blindness.
I want
to live here,
stay pure.
Cloud-
confounded.

Condensation tracks along the grimy slope
of the plastic ceiling,
drips on a young couple.
Alerted,
the flight attendant explains
the thinness of the plane's metal skin,
how freezing the air outside
at thirty-five thousand feet, how ice
gradually works its way in.
Through the gaps.

We do it all the time,
rodeo-ride the dichotomy
of safe and unsafe —
snap at the spouse, hand over the credit card
heart in mouth, reckon we're right to drive.
We are the accident-free,

stepping airily over the gap
between cabin

               and floating stair.

Perfect fit

Fidgeting burns calories, reveals *The Australian*.
Light bulb – so much explained:

why I, my father, uncles, aunts
all foot-tapping, finger-rapping, lip-chewing fidgeters,

remain skinny as greyhounds: we're easily bored.
Why Australian kids are overweight: clearly, it's

the rising standard of education. Everything is transmuted.
Commercial breaks: a community service,

the doctor's waiting room: the new gym. A dark secret.
The length of your wait could be inversely proportional

to your cholesterol level. Treatment by neglect.
Capitalism, though, won't keep you waiting –

there'll be half-hour Fidget classes between Step and Pilates,
digital fidgetometers to track your progress,

and at three in the morning, slick infomercials for
the Fidgetron 4000. Take heart, you students

of accounting and law, and you noble souls
suffering through bad poetry readings –

a bored audience is a fit audience!

Habanera-sinuous

Urbane, you coax the jazz from its cushy armchair,
charm, subvert, chuck it off a cliff in style.

Centred in the drums' taut mandala, your smile floats —
these days, wrists and calves check back in with you
only periodically and this paroles you, grooves you in
at the ganglion. Co-ordination's tedium and tongue-pinch —
stuff you left on one of several possible beaches years ago:

now the dancer's rhythm
creates you star-like, as if body weight
were a trad mass delusion, and to prove it
your pelvis centrifuges at a quantum point,
indefinable over its tangible stool.
The beat is Jonah swallowed by finesse.

Your self-possession is op art even to you,
your cunning mechanics no longer traceable
as your head turns away and down,
removing itself, superfluous perhaps,
or repositioning its ear. Swinging,

you hint, calibrate, explode another wave
with all the pert control of cool — no overspray
splashes frocks, no kickboard is hammered
in the synaesthetic wash. Today, Habanera-sinuous,
the merest shoulder-roll belies your magnetism.

On This, My Forty-Fifth Yeare

I take within mine purview mine Demesne,
Mine Fielde, mine Lamb and Bulloc, mine unpaide Mortgage,
Mine Offspringe, fair as swete Sumer's cuccu, tho she playeth
Loudely the J-poppe, and speketh moste excessively
Of Minecrafte; and sum change in my Selfe I detecte:
Dismayede I am by fulle Moustache untrimm'd,
While Eyebrow-haire with stunning Spede I loseth,
A little Fatte; and for my noble Stede
The auto gearbox chooseth.
But soft! Mine Love still groweth, bright as Morne,
Mine Witt, mine Courage, tho I weare the daggie shoeoe
Which it doth shame mine Childe to walk beside;
With Faith, with Comp'ny, fulle many a grace possess'd,
And moste: Bleste with true Friendes. I love you All.

Backyard snail

I lift you to eye level. Both your eyes,
dark flower buds on sinew stems,
look into mine. There is a fairground hilarity
to eyes on stalks:

as if to prove it, I waggle a finger
in front of them. Stately, you ignore this
until I drop my hand, and its quick shadow
falling across your vision triggers fear:

each eye-stalk whips inward
fast as the cord on my vacuum cleaner,
your long head shrinks back, frilly-edged,
a cabbage growing in reverse

and I laugh.
You're a silent comedy I have hurried past a thousand times.

Later I will be amazed to learn
your lifespan is ten to fifteen years.
Suddenly you are valuable –
how many times have you done this work

of eating, sleeping, moving on?
You're a show regardless of audience,
a full house,
your scribble of trails, morning reviews of your travels.

Your head emerges, and it makes me glad
to see that head, intent with lettuce dreams.
You are a touchstone, telling me: keep on,
    enjoy the world, in all its tiny bites.

Like aeons, like women

It is her diffidence that first delights me —
no startle reflex, no recoil from my sight.

Fine turtle neck, her sinewed, wavelet flippers
wholly elegant, glowing green and cream

under the water on which I'm cast like an oil slick.
The clear regard of her scaled, mild eye

makes my breath catch — she is that rarest of animals,
the one without a human-damaged history

and is going through the water to be a mother,
to farewell her ecstatic, pliant-shelled eggs.

I know what it is
to be drawn to reproduction: I think of the eggs

in water in my own body, of the poet
who, after her mother's funeral, stood under the shower

as ceremony on taking the matriarch's mantle.
I fear we will collide, and she is big —

but she makes the merest ducking of her head,
and I watch her baroque shell

glide just under my belly,
as close as the breath I hold, then rise again

and go straight on, leaving me baptised,
fecund, wondering

as I watch her flippers cycle
like aeons, like women.

Mammogram in the time of coronavirus

You can't imagine the sumo stance,
the wrestler's knot of limbs bent and grasping and wrapped
around platform and handle; the press to my breastbone
recalls what's lost to me – hugging friends and family.
We do the still pose together,
stop breathing now dear, stop breathing;
the machine revolves its night and day
around my Copernican moon. We view the image:
breast as bomb,
black and white moon-landing footage
threatening as breathless space. I want it to be as empty,
and when the doctor comes to talk to me, I stop breathing
again. I walk free, paper towel to the door handle
with my body of asymptomatic secrets,
covid, gravid, rabid – all the things I could be,
but today am not, wrestling in my mind;
grateful for breath, the praise in the dark curve's beauty.

A Chinese whisper

My smallest fingernail
curves up now at one edge.
It's the cellular thing, I suppose –
having to copy yourself every seven years
mistakes creep in. My blueprint
in unreliable hands. Shrug, human error.
The nail lifts like a joy or an uprising:
I'm a dented pie-tin, a Chinese whisper.

The ocean in your briefcase
for Peter

I didn't know what corporate communications
were, but you hired me, green, fifteen. Your handwritten work
typed daily by my hungry mind.

Larrikin from the halls of Canberra –
the first adult I'd known who, in the face of problems, said
now, let's think about this. And I listened to you think –

parenting, in a way: on journalism, politics,
negotiation, art, your poster of Hokusai's *Wave*.
When I wrote the slogan for Hobart

and won, you told me how to address
the Lord Mayor; when I cried,
unable to afford a house, you lent me money.

I followed you through marriages and mergers.
I never saw you dripping, stripped to the waist
half out of your cold wetsuit (Friday *board meetings*) –

I saw the sand in your Jag, the calm you brought back,
your musculature buttoned in shirt and tie,
the linen jacket you called your Richie Benaud.

I took from you insistence on fine writing
and its flip side: your love for poking fun at it all.
Your pride in your son, playing me his songs,

and how you shook when his baby nearly drowned.
How to bowl a googly, down the heritage hallway
of our offices. You kissed me as a bride.

Joyful over my publishing deal, I call the number etched in memory —
dead. On Facebook, I find your ashes.
Today at my book launch: your grin, your absence in the room.

Blinded from blue to blue

Tack. Scuttle like a sluiced insect, port to starboard.
Toe the inch of southern ocean slopping against the boat's bones.
Grow quickly ashamed of your clumsy feet
stripped of ground, clinging dumbly to sodden toe straps,
your fingers scrabbling for purchase
along a seamless brink of caulk.

Gybe. Scramble. Keep your head down. This cantilever boom,
five inches through, has its head. In perfidious wind
the sail snaps out like an airbag,
hardwood slamming through 180 degrees
will flick you into space. Let's be clear:
no Mae Wests for guests.

Speed gathers, exponentiates. Your splashed face dries in salt,
the boat lurches:
here is where the faith comes in.

                        Lean out.

                              Let go

of landlocked notions of gravity and vertices —
here your toes are sufficient to hold you,
anchor your body's calling as torque and ballast.
Think freely. Think knots and hydroplanes. Lean out.
Seek the fulcrum point
of boat's edge under thigh.

                   Weigh against the wind
                   your heart's construction,

                             test the kinetics of mettle.
You must not think on the depth, the quick cold swallow;
think on velocity, slant boards, your natant levitation.

Flick your salt-dazzled gaze over the sail's curve,
past it to a sky which defies focal length. Tilt your ear to the wash
boiling below your taut suspending,
the whites of your eyes to the thralled slash
where sea and sky converge and vaporise.
Hear physics buck and coil, as if, having dared this much,

you could slip alive from one blue into the other
untouched
slick as wet rope looping through a palm.

And now you taste the madness
in sailors' whispers. Let sun turn your eyes to diamonds.
How lovely to let yourself be courted,
blinded from blue to blue,
look up and up, grow punch-drunk with horizons,

dream, topple like an angel,
drown in sky.

Memoir of water

From toddlerhood: a memory of careful bending
and plashing my baby hand in the Huon's edge.
My childhood learning held in a saltwater brain;
my solitary mother walking her babies by the river.

Swimming with friends last summer, our bodies
larger with age, remade into squealing children.
Floating in night's bay as the fireworks
scribbled joy on a black sky, black rippled waves.

The turbid water that followed my baby out.
The tender water I washed my child in.
In my home town, water's coldness, its finger-thrill.
My paper-boat poem, rose petals for the dead.

How many times water has heard my sorrows.
It never leaves me, willing to take me in.
Give me its power to daily lift through cloud —
its clean forgetfulness that engenders courage.

Acknowledgements

Poems in this collection have been published, some in slightly different forms, in *Thirty Australian Poets (UQP), The Weekend Australian, The Sun Herald, Australian Poetry Anthology, Communion Arts Journal, Meanjin, Heat, Blue Dog: Australian Poetry, Blue Giraffe, Small Packages, Sweet Mammalian, Famous Reporter, The Poets' Republic, Island Story: Tasmania in object and text (Text Publishing), Writing Water: Rain, River, Reef (Red Room Poetry), In Your Hands anthology (Red Room Poetry), Oral History Association of Australia journal, Grieve.* The poems *Blazer* and *Ocean nocturne* were commissioned by Red Room Poetry and published on their website. *Hope of escape* was commissioned by Tasmania's Festival of Voices. *Backyard snail* was commissioned by the Tasmanian Poetry Festival. The line "one... a fool, the other a fool" is by Sylvia Plath. The poem *On this, my Forty-fifth Yeare* is after John Clarke. The title of this book is that of a poem by Elizabeth Bishop.

Triptych was shortlisted in the Montreal International Poetry Prize 2020. *Light, water* and *The ocean in your briefcase* were shortlisted in the Bridport Prize 2020. *Roy, 1932 (part i)* won the Tom Collins Poetry Prize 2009. *Blinded from Blue to Blue* won First Prize in the Tasmanian Literary Awards 2006.

SUPPORTED BY

This project was assisted through Arts Tasmania by the Minister for the Arts. It was also assisted by a Fellowship at Varuna, the Writers' House.

Tasmanian Government

Thank you to John Foulcher, David Musgrave, Lyn Reeves, Kim Nolan, Tim Slade, Peter Bishop, Judy Johnson and Sarah Day.

Esther Ottaway is an award-winning Australian poet. She has been published widely over twenty years in literary journals around the world including *Rattle* (US), leading newspapers including *The Australian* and *The Canberra Times*, and anthologies, notably the acclaimed *Thirty Australian Poets* (UQP).

In 2020 Esther was shortlisted for the Montreal International and Bridport Poetry Prizes. Her awards include a Fellowship at Varuna, the Writers' House, as well as grants for arts practise from the Australia Council, Sidney Myer Foundation, Arts Tasmania and Regional Arts. A former Board member of *Island* magazine, Esther has written commissioned performance poetry works for the stage for the Adelaide Cabaret Festival and Tasmania's Festival of Voices and worked collaboratively with artists in other forms, including visual arts and fibre arts.

Works from her book *Blood Universe: poems on pregnancy*, anthologised in national and international collections on parenthood, are recognised as an important exploration of women's experience. Poems from this book have been listed as further reading in *60 Classic Australian Poems*, set to music for the Tasmanian Symphony Orchestra, and featured on ABC Radio National.

Her next poetry collection, *She Doesn't Seem Autistic*, will explore the experiences of women and girls on the autism spectrum. Esther lives in Hobart.

www.ingramcontent.com/pod-product-compliance
Lightning Source LLC
Chambersburg PA
CBHW030850090426
42737CB00009B/1177